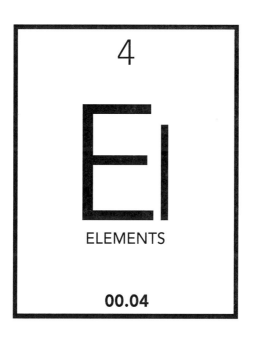

Second edition Copyright © 2015 Lighthouse Church

Written by Paul Foster Jr.

Cover and Book Design by Jesse Freeman and Shelley Hull

ISBN 10: 1632960397

ISBN 13: 978-1-63296-039-9

eISBN 10: 1632960400

eISBN 13: 978-1-63296-040-5

Printed in the United States of America

This book is dedicated to Lighthouse Church.

It is one of the greatest joys of my
life to chase after Jesus with you.

Love you guys.

1	2
Tr Truth	**Wp** Worship
23.41	43.63
3	4
Cm Community	**Ms** Mission
65.81	83.103

Contents

"It is not a daily increase, but a daily decrease.

Hack away at the inessentials."

- Bruce Lee

Prologue

Si

SIMPLEXITY

7.21

I like simplicity.

Actually, let me rephrase that.

I *love* simplicity!

Part of the reason I love simplicity is just me being who I am. I mean, typically I want to get to the bare bones of just about everything as fast as possible. And I've always been that way (just ask my mom!). I hate clutter, I purge like it's cool, and I can't stand any kind of excess.

I also love simplicity because it's what I would call an "occupational necessity." Now that I've been blessed to be a pastor of a growing church, there are flat out not enough hours in the day to get everything done. As such, I've found that it's generally in everybody's best interests for me to get to the bottom line as soon as reasonably possible. I look at most issues that come across my desk as a kind of challenge to see how efficiently I can strip them down to their most simplified form. Actually, in self-defense, I've turned "getting to the bottom line" into a kind of game.[1] In doing so, I've found the process of simplifying

> *Simplicity is the management of complexity...it's as straightforward as just removing everything that's unnecessary.*

invariably helps me better understand a particular issue, and many times this same process can help me better explain the issue to someone else.

See, simplicity is not just the absence of complexity. Many times, simplicity is more the art of *managing* the complexity of an idea or a situation. This is big because some things will always be complex.

For example, the complex system behind electrical power has a lot to do with conductors, transformers, and

---

1. This is because the alternative would probably be to lose my mind. Seriously.

electrons whizzing around. But for my needs, it's much less complicated. Do the lights come on when I throw the switch and will my phone charge over night? Simple.

Complex question: What are the chemical properties of latex emulsions and wall coverings? Simple version: Will this paint last more than a week and a half in my kids' bedroom?

Complex topic: The United States budget deficit, which was a whopping $620 billion in 2013 alone. (That's crazy!) Simplified version? How about we stop spending money that we don't have? See how easy this is?

Complex topic: women. Simple version? Okay, so maybe that's not all that great of an example, but you get the point. *Simplicity is the management of complexity.*

So, how do you actually manage complexity? It's as straightforward as just removing everything that's unnecessary. With our finite minds that are prone to overload, a big part of simplicity is the "less-is-more mindset." This allows you to recognize and rid yourself of those things that are not necessary to achieve your mission. Now, if you've ever actually tried this, you already know it takes a lot of practice, and it takes a lot of discipline to really walk out a "less-is-more" mindset. But in the 24/7 marketing freak-fest that defines the twenty-first century, practicing "less-is-more" for me is "less" of a philosophy and "more" of a survival strategy.

Here's another thing about simplicity: it can be elusive. I mean, for real, if it's so easy to achieve, why don't more people live simply? I can't even begin to recount how many people I've heard over the past few years say, "I just wanna simplify my life." In response to this often heartfelt cry, I generally ask them, "And what does simplifying your life look like to you?" And, of course, it means different things to different people, but typically I hear:

- I want to reduce my debt (great idea!)
- I want to declutter my house (I couldn't agree more!)
- I want to purge my schedule of meaningless things (amen!)

- I'd like to get out of this marriage (whoops, hold up now…)
- I want to get back to what matters in life (love it!)

And so again, *reduction* is a common theme in the pursuit of simplicity. Another way of saying this is… simplicity often has much more to do with subtraction than it does with addition. It's kind of ironic, but in this age of information abundance, technological overload, and a million and one choices in everything from tee shirts to TOMS, those who experience life to the fullest are – ready? – **those who learn what to leave out so they can concentrate on what's really important.**

Okay, now here's where it gets good! This idea of simplicity is central to the message and life of Jesus! And this is sort of a big deal!

"Why?" you might ask.

> *Those who experience life to the fullest are those who learn what to leave out so they can concentrate on what's really important.*

Here's why – because Jesus is the creator and author of all of life, of everything visible and invisible. Everything from the smallest subatomic particles to the immeasurable universe itself was personally created by Him. On top of that, He was the architect of life itself, and He created it in His infinite wisdom. The prophet Isaiah reminds us that the thoughts of Jesus are so far above ours, that it's like trying to measure the distance between sea level and deep space![2] It can't be done! Yet this same Jesus, who created everything we know about (which is probably not all that much actually) and everything we *don't* know about (which is probably quite a bit, when you think about it) came and physically lived among us. Why?

He came to demonstrate how much He loves us and to give us an example of how we should live our lives. Jesus established a kingdom built on the two commands of love for God and love for neighbor.

Given all that, you'd probably think that in the brief 33 years that Jesus spent on this earth, He would have had to

---

2. Isaiah 5:8

work at a furious pace to somehow jam in all the teaching, healing and setting the record straight that He intended to accomplish. This is especially true because His ministry only lasted 36 months – yet that 36 months forever changed the world.

So, it must have been a frantic 36 months, right?

Frenzied. Sort of hectic?

Actually, the Gospel writers paint a picture of anything *but* a frantic, frenzied or hectic life. We see Jesus living life *simply*. He welcomed children to sit

> *We see Jesus living simply.*

with Him, and He spent a great deal of time talking with His friends. Never do we see Him operating at a frantic pace. We see that He deeply understood the need for His children to live in simplicity. He was the absolute Master at distilling hopelessly tangled-up emotional, religious and spiritual complexities into simple, easy to understand elements – the same way He does today. Many of His solutions involved child-like faith and simple humility – the same way they do today. And as the richest Being we can possibly imagine,

Who owns all things everywhere and for all time[3] – there has never been anyone who possibly demonstrated a less-is-more attitude better than the King of the Universe, Who came to earth quietly, humbly and in submission to the will of His Father.

So, this small book outlines four simple elements as demonstrated in the life of Jesus that not only liberate us but lead us to life and a life more abundant. Jesus was very straightforward when He made the offer to "Come to me, all you who are weary and burdened, and I will give you rest. Take my yoke upon you, and learn from me, for I am gentle and humble in heart, and you will find rest for your souls. For my yoke is easy and my burden is light."[4] This simple statement encourages me that Jesus is much more about "decluttering"

> *In His divine subtraction, He tells us what we are to focus on. Ultimately, we learn that we are to focus on Him alone.*

---

3. Psalm 50:9-12

4. Matthew 11:28-30

our lives than adding to what we need to do. **The gospel of Jesus is so simple!** In His divine subtraction, He tells us what we are to focus on. Ultimately, we learn that we are to focus on Him alone.

So, just what exactly did Jesus, as the undisputed Master of simplicity, focus on during His ministry? Jesus' ministry can be summarized in four distinct elements, and not coincidentally these are the same four elements on which Lighthouse Church concentrates. It's how we try – by God's grace! – to keep Lighthouse a simple church focused simply on Jesus. These four elements are:

Truth. Jesus was a crusader for truth. Eventually, He identified Himself as the Truth![5] He constantly emphasized truth because He knew how prone we are to be led astray by lies, lies that lead us to harm and lies that can lead to devastation and destruction. By contrast, Jesus leads us not only to life but to a far better and more abundant life. Jesus is the Truth.

――――――――
5. John 14:6

Worship. Everything Jesus did was to glorify His Father. He did nothing on His own accord, and neither did He have His own agenda. In humility, He submitted only to the will of His Father in heaven. He demonstrated a life of worship in everything that He did and in anything He put His hand to by maintaining constant communication and a reverent respect towards His Father. This is, of course, exactly what we're created for; a worshipful relationship with our Creator. And just in case you're thinking, "Well, I'm not really that much of a worshipper…" Don't worry, it's really not a question of *if* we will worship; we're hardwired to worship already. The question is – *what* will we worship?

Community. Jesus was, no doubt, a man of the people and functioned within the community. Certainly, He would have had the right to live in solitude if He chose, maybe issuing instructions and orders to His disciples from some secluded spot and healing a fortunate few who might dare approach Him. Instead, He was embedded in and among people, completely approachable, ministering to them and continually serving their needs. Why? Because He loved them, and was eager to include them in His family. He knew that people were the "name of the game," and His mission was to create a community that was full of life – abundant life.

Mission. During His entire ministry, one thing Jesus never lost sight of was His mission. The Bible clearly portrays a Savior who did exactly what His Father required, exactly on time and in exactly the right way. He lived according to mission, served according to mission and when the proper time came, He actually *died* according to mission. What an example!

And what was His mission? He was sent to the lost sheep of Israel, to reach the lost and to make disciples. At the same time, He was sent to die on our behalf, to pay the penalty for our sins and provide a way back to the Father. This is something we could never do for ourselves. And in obedience to Him, this is exactly what the mission of LHC is: to reach the lost and make disciples[6], because He commanded us to do so in the Gospels.

──────────

6. Matthew 28:19-20

Now, here's the deal. These four elements are not just truths about Jesus, impressive as that might be. They should be increasingly true of us as well. These four elements that were priorities of Jesus must become priorities of the modern day disciple. So, as we work through this small book, I want to tell you how exciting and mind-blowing it is to watch Jesus work out His will through us here at the Lighthouse and throughout His church all over the world.

Neither church life nor discipleship should be complicated. It's simple, it's proven, and it's incredibly liberating. When we understand the need for simplicity as demonstrated by Jesus and when we look at complex issues through the simplicity of God's truth, then by the power of the Holy Spirit, we can begin subtracting those things from our lives which are harmful or just unnecessary which makes us more and more available to participate in the mission of Jesus.

So here's my question, are you ready to explore those four simple elements that Jesus lived out during His ministry?

Then let's do the dang thing!

"The truth is incontrovertible. Malice may attack it, ignorance

may deride it, but in the end, there it is."

- Winston Churchill

In the spring of AD 33 a confrontation took place in Jerusalem between a relatively obscure Roman prefect named Pontius Pilate and a seemingly inconsequential Jewish peasant known as Jesus of Nazareth. Jesus had been accused of treason against Caesar – strangely enough not by the Romans but by a coalition of religious authorities. Before having Him tortured, Pilate took the opportunity to interrogate Jesus and asked Him if He considered Himself to be a king. "You say that I am a king. In fact, the reason I was born and came into the world is to testify to the truth. Everyone on the side of truth listens to Me," was the astonishing reply of the

Nazarene. An unimpressed Pilate responded, "What is the truth?"[1]

It's an extremely interesting question which has been around for quite some time. Two ancient Greek philosophers, Plato and Aristotle, disagreed on many issues, but they *did* agree on a simple definition of truth: Truth is *"that which corresponds with reality."*[2]

For more than 1,500 years, scholars accepted this seemingly reasonable definition as the foundation of sound reasoning. Based upon it, in the Middle Ages, philosophers and theologians like Anselm of Canterbury (1033 – 1109) and Thomas Aquinas (1225 – 1274) built complex systems of logically connected propositions designed to prove the rationality of the Christian faith. Seems a bit intense, but that's what they were into. Their work influenced the generations that followed to think of truth primarily in terms of propositions.[3]

---

1. John 18:37-38

2. Karsten Frils Johansen, A History of Ancient Philosophy: From the Beginning to Augustine (New York: Routledge 2005), 317.

3. A *proposition* is a statement, usually in the form of a sentence, which is either true or false. For instance, "Paul Foster is a man" is a proposition.

A couple of centuries later, the Protestant Reformation challenged[4] many of the propositions of the Roman Catholic Church which eventually led to an all-out religious war. Christians began murdering other Christians who did not agree with their understanding of truth, both sides believing they were serving Jesus by doing so.

Crazy, right?

Eventually, people came to their senses, stopped killing each other and reasoned that if the Christians couldn't agree on what propositions were true from the Bible, then there must be some other way of knowing the truth. This led to another philosopher, Rene Descartes, to argue that we cannot actually be certain of the truth. The only thing that we know to be true is that we exist. His famous axiom was, *"I think, therefore I am."*[5] Though he didn't intend it, Descartes' idea eventually led to something called "subjectivism." Subjectivism is the idea that "I, the subject" am the one who

---

4. To put it politely.

5. Rene Descartes, Discourse on the Method Part IV

determines what's right, what's wrong, what's true and what's not – without submitting my judgment to any authority outside myself.

Not good.

In other words, truth depends on me, the individual, ultimately allowing each person to determine truth in his or her own mind.

While at face value you'd think that is an empowering way of looking at things, this line of thinking has a foundational problem. If the truth can be different for each person, then absolute truth doesn't really exist. We only have opinion and preference. And, of course, this is precisely where we are today. Truth in this culture has fallen on hard times. In 2006, noted Christian evangelist and commentator Chuck Colson wrote that a full 63 percent of Americans **do not believe in an objective truth at all.** This is beyond crazy!

What's more alarming, his statistics also reveal that *53 percent of self-professing evangelicals* don't believe in an objective truth either.[6] Consequently, we find ourselves living

6. George Barna, quoted in "Emerging Confusion", Christianity Today, www.christianitytoday.com

in a day and age in which the majority of people (including *a majority of Christians)* are wandering around trying to get a fix on what the truth is!

If they're not lost in a fog of subjectivism, then many are equally confused by something called "relativism." This doctrine holds that truth exists *only in relation to a culture or society*. Simply put, there's no such thing as an absolute truth; truth depends on what the culture, at the time, deems to be true. What seems true for one time or culture might not be true for another.

Errors like subjectivism and relativism are the mantras often promoted by the popular "experts" and sources to whom tons of people look to for guidance in life. I'm talking about the likes of Dr. Phil, Oprah Winfrey, People Magazine, Judge Judy, Joel Osteen, the Huffington Post, David Letterman and probably Kanye for all I know. People look to these authorities in a desperate attempt to find the truth. Sometimes people turn to other religious writings like the Koran or to Hollywood-inspired mysticism like Kabbalah or bizarre cults like Scientology. The underlying assumption seems to be that if you dump enough opinion into a large enough pot and then mix it up thoroughly, a reasonable person should be able to find "truth."

It's sort of the modern day version of the Indian parable of the blind men and the elephant, famously retold by the American poet John Saxe. In the parable, five blind men stumble upon an elephant in the woods. In attempting to describe it, each provides his own personal (but limited) perspective. One man grabbing its huge leg describes the elephant as a tree while another grabs its trunk and insists the elephant is more like a snake; the man holding on to its tail insists it's exactly like a rope and so on. Oftentimes this parable is used to make the case that no one has the lock on truth, and that truth depends upon the perspective and interpretation of the individual.

What is usually missed in this parable is not that the truth lies in the unique perspective of each man, but that *the men describing the elephant are blind! BLIND!* How ironic. Of course, this is the big problem with subjectivism and relativism. Both of them are textbook examples of the blind leading the blind. Oddly enough, the question that never quite gets answered is, "How can I be certain that my opinion (subjectivism) or cultural values (relativism) are correct and truthful?"

The answer is, "On your own, you can't!"

Fortunately, the Bible takes the complete opposite stance to both of these false ideologies. The inspired authors of Scripture were confident that truth **does** in fact exist, *and that truth exists apart from any man's opinion.* This is a shocker for a lot of people, but nevertheless, it comes straight from the Bible.

A reasonable person might ask at this point, "Well, why all the hype? Does truth even matter?" The answer is a resounding, "YES!" and here's why: *what you believe ultimately*

> *What you believe ultimately determines how you behave.*

determines how you behave. Read that again until it sinks in. I'll wait. Actually, because I know you're probably not going to do that, let me just restate it for your convenience. ***What you believe ultimately determines how you behave.***

This principle will always play out. Example: what you believe about the sanctity of life will determine how you treat those around you, unborn or otherwise. Likewise, what you believe about the importance of giving will determine whether you're a cheerful giver or the stingiest person on the planet.[7] What you believe about your obligation as an employee will play a major role in how hard you work for your boss. And what you believe about your husband or wife has a lot to do with whether your home is either a refuge or more like a battlefield. Ultimately, what you believe about reality, about life, and about its purpose will factor into how you live your life. Truth is important!

> *Truth is absolutely absolute and absolutely unchanging.*

So given its critical importance, we should breathe a collective sigh of relief that the Bible teaches that truth is definitely *not* relative. Truth is not subject to man's whims, because man didn't create truth. Truth is not a matter of human opinion, because our Sovereign Creator didn't need our input in constructing it. And truth does not vary from culture to culture or from age to age, because it was formed and set before the foundations of the universe. Truth is absolutely absolute

---

7. Okay, I'm exaggerating here, but for some of you, not by much. You know who you are.

and absolutely unchanging. (Dang that's a lot of absolutin'!) What's more, despite the enormity of the concept, God allows truth to be actually *known* by mankind. In a culture that doesn't seem to know the difference between up and down, this is fantastic news!

"Okay then," you ask in a reasonable tone, "how can truth be known?"

Great question.

The answer is that God has revealed truth to us in three different ways.

> *Actually, everything in all creation points to the truth of God's wisdom and authority and glorifies its Creator.*

God Shows Truth

If we want to find truth, the Scriptures tell us to begin by looking up at the sky. Yes, the sky. Psalm 19 says that the heavens declare the glory of God, that the sheer mind-blowing splendor of the world by day and the brilliance of the stars by night is evidence of the power of the Creator.[8] If the outside

––––––––––

8. Obviously my paraphrase.

doesn't impress you, then just take a look inside. The human body is an incredible display of His wisdom; the mere fact that your brain allows you to sit and contemplate or paint pictures with your thoughts only further points to His greatness. The complexity of our genetic makeup even leaves some of the world's greatest scientists utterly amazed. *Everything* in all of creation points to the truth of God's wisdom and authority and glorifies its Creator. When we consider the vastness of the universe, we gain an even greater appreciation for the greatness of God revealed in King Solomon's declaration, "Behold, heaven and the highest heaven cannot contain you."[9]

> *The entire universe is proclaiming His greatness, His glory and His incredible power, 24/7.*

God showing Himself through this revelation is His blessing to a doubtful and hostile world. This makes truth a kind of proclamation. The entire universe is proclaiming His greatness, His glory and His incredible power, 24/7. Romans 1:20 tells us in no uncertain terms that "since

---

9. 1 Kings 8:27

the creation of the world God's invisible qualities – his eternal power and divine nature – **have been clearly seen**, being understood from what has been made, so that people are without excuse."

At this point you might be asking the question, "If truth is revealed in creation, then why do things seem so perverse, wicked, whacked-out, violent and jacked-up on this planet?" The Apostle Paul answers this exact question when he says, "The wrath of God is being revealed from heaven against all godlessness and wickedness of men, *who suppress the truth by their wickedness…* and though they claimed to be wise, they became fools, *and exchanged the truth of God for a lie.*"[10] Simply put, Paul says that the truth is seen clearly in what God has created, but people have suppressed and perverted that truth. It's not that truth is lacking – **it's that we have chosen to reject it**.

Walk into a home where there's fighting and strife, and I will guarantee you that truth does not reign there. Witness a government that is unjust and oppressive of its

_____

10. Romans 1:18-23

people and you'll see a government that is a stranger to truth. Our culture is infatuated with money and sex instead of wisdom and understanding, and as a result, our marriages are falling apart, our families are disintegrating and our nation is teetering on economic collapse. The examples are endless, but you get the point – truth is of absolutely critical importance.

God Speaks the Truth

The Bible also assures us that "all Scripture is given by inspiration of God, and is profitable for doctrine, for reproof, for correction, for instruction in righteousness, so that the man of God may be complete, and thoroughly equipped for every good work."[11] As you can see, you get a lot of goodies from Scripture. God spoke through Israel's prophets in the Old Testament and Jesus' earliest disciples in the New Testament in order to give us a written record of the truth. It's a unique, God-inspired account of how the Creator sees

---

11. 2 Timothy 3:16-17

reality. And amazingly, we get to read it! Like, right now if you want to! And when we read and study God's word, we are given the incredible opportunity to see the world through His eyes as expressed through His words.

In Psalm 119 (which is basically 176 verses of God speaking to us about the truth of the Scriptures), the author states in verse 160,

> *"The entirety of Your word is truth, and every one of Your righteous judgments endures forever."*

This is exactly why Jesus prayed in His high priestly prayer, "Father, sanctify them by your Word," before adding, "**Your Word is truth**."[12] This is awesome! The Holy Scriptures provide us a look at the very nature of God. We get to see what He's like, what He requires and what our future holds as followers of Jesus. And get this: **all of it's true!** At the same time, the Word changes us, molds us, convicts us, stirs us and increases the God-given faith within us.

C'mon now! You tell me, what's not to love?

———————

12. John 17:17

God Comes

While both creation and the Bible are sources of truth that would have easily satisfied Pilate's question, it's as heart-breaking as it is profound that the embodiment of absolute truth was standing right in front of him… and he didn't recognize it.

The revelation that Pilate so sadly missed was that the man he would condemn to death was nothing short of the pinnacle of all understanding, the reason for history itself, the very Author and Finisher of all creation and the answer to all of our questions. This man was no inconsequential Jewish peasant but rather, the One who created us for His good pleasure in the first place.

> *This is because Truth is a Person, and His name is Jesus.*

The Bible assures us this One wasn't just *at* the beginning. He *is* the beginning.[13]

We're told that He didn't just create the universe, but

13. John 1:1

He's actively holding it all together.[14] It tells us that He won't simply be present at the end or can sort of see the end, but that somehow He *is* the end.[15] Finally, it states that He not only understands the point of everything that will transpire throughout our lives and in this world, but that He, in fact, *is* the point of our lives![16] This is because Truth is a Person. His name is Jesus.

Don't take my word for it. Jesus Himself said, "I am the Way, I am the Truth, and I am the Life."[17] Another truly game-changing statement! But, without the Spirit of God to convict us and teach us (sometimes quickly and sometimes gradually) of the absolute trustworthiness of these words, I doubt we would ever get our heads around them.

> *He is the Life we've been searching for all along.*

Yet, for those of us who have tried other ways and then have finally come to Him, we understand perfectly well

---

14. Colossians 1:17

15. Revelation 22:13

16. Colossians 1:18

17. John 14:6

that He is in fact *The Way*. Some of us have searched for truth, some of us have run from the truth and some of us might have even tried to invent alternate truths along the way, only to come up woefully short and realize – *Jesus* is the *Truth*. So many out there are desperately searching for life, as though it were an experience or an accomplishment, a sunset on a beach or some random number in a bank account. Instead, as it turns out, He is the *Life* we've been searching for all along.

How can that be? It's because **Truth is a Person**, the very Person who created us. And by some unwarranted miracle of God's grace, we're permitted to know Him personally.[18] And once you know Jesus and experience Truth firsthand, then everything – and I mean *everything* – changes. Knowing the Truth liberates us and sets us free. Truth becomes – instead of some abstract concept – a way of living, and a way of being, and a way of walking through life. Truth becomes a way of thinking, and a way of loving other people, and of seeing, and of serving.

Wow.

---

18. As in, personally.

<u>Think About It.</u>

1. How is Pilate's question, "What is truth?" echoed in our culture today?

2. What are some examples or consequences of looking at truth as relative or subjective?

3. Considering the topic of truth, what perspective does Psalm 119:105 lend by stating, "Your word is a lamp for my feet, a light for my path"?

4. What are the implications of Jesus not only knowing truth but actually being "the Way, the Truth, the Life" (John 14:6)?

5. How would you answer if someone from our culture asked Pilate's question, "What is truth?"

"Many Spirit-filled authors have exhausted the thesaurus in order to describe God with the glory He deserves. His perfect holiness, by definition, assures us that our words can't contain Him. Isn't it a comfort to worship a God we cannot exaggerate?"

- Francis Chan, Crazy Love

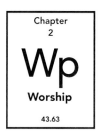

Given the incredible truths we encountered in the previous chapter – that God shows us His glory through His creation, that God speaks to us through the gift of the Scriptures and finally, that God actually came to us in the Person of Jesus Christ – what should man's response be?

Bluntly stated, man's response should be to worship Jesus.

But first we must ask, "what is worship?" Worship can mean a myriad of things to a myriad of people. And as I say that, I know that many people might even be convinced that worship is an antequated religious practice that has no impact on our modern day life. Other people, with the best of intentions, have a sort of half-baked picture of what worship means in their minds. This picture might be based on various bits and pieces of what they've heard about worship through the years, or it might be based on what they've experienced during a church service or seen on television. People struggle to put all these pieces together, trying to make sense of the concept of worship, because they have very likely *way*, way overcomplicated it.

Let's take a look at what worship is, and why it's one of the four elements of Lighthouse Church.

The Origins of Worship

First, worship is not a new practice. It's not something that came into its own in recent times or suddenly popped up during some Pentecostal movement back in the 70's. Worship dates all the way back to the very beginning of human history. Archeologists have discovered ancient ruins and cave walls that prominently portray worship as part of the everyday life of some of the earliest civilizations we know of, civilizations such as the Kingdom of Assyria or the Babylonian Empire. Even earlier civilizations that flourished in Mesopotamia practiced not just individual worship, but community worship as well with people gathering in one location to pay homage to their various gods by bowing down and bringing gifts. And most of the time when people think of worship, this is what they picture: people prostrating themselves before some deity, and sacrificing some cow or ox that happened to be in the wrong place at the wrong time. Or more modernly, a room full of people shouting and singing with their hands raised to the sky. But whether you look at history or the present, you will find people worshiping.

This is because God invented worship. This invention can be traced back to the origins of humanity in the Old Testament. The Scriptures clearly show us how God taught mankind to come and gather to pray and to lift their voices in acts of praise that even included the sacrifice of animals to atone for their sin. This helps explain why all people tend to assemble together, pray up a storm and then offer sacrifices even to man-made and truly horrific gods like Baal, Ashtoreth, Chemosh, Dagon, and a whole thoroughly unpleasant host of others dating back thousands of years. This innate tendency of people to worship seems to be hardwired into human beings from way back.

What is Worship?

To understand why we worship, let's first look at what comprises worship. The Apostle Paul offers us a very clear look at the God's-eye view of worship from the Book of Romans Chapter 11:36 and Chapter 12:1. Here's what he writes,

For from him and through him and for him are all things. To him be the glory forever! Amen.

It's a simple but very profound concept. Paul states bluntly that God created all things <u>from</u> Himself, that everything that was created was done so <u>through</u> His power and that He created everything ultimately <u>for</u> Himself.

Probably feeling the overwhelming coolness of the whole thing, Paul follows this statement with the very appropriate, "to him be the glory forever!" and closes the whole chapter out with a rousing holla: "Amen!" And although some of us use that word all the time, it's worth noting the word "amen" comes from an ancient Hebrew word which translates "to believe."[1] So, when Paul (or you or me, for that matter) busts out with an "amen" in casual conversation, (or me while preaching) it means, "YES, I believe that!" Talk about highly appropriate.

Next, Paul takes it a step further and goes on to verse 1 of chapter 12, explaining exactly how we should respond to the profound truth of God's amazing nature that we just read about in chapter 11. He writes,

Therefore, I urge you, brothers and sisters, in view of God's mercy, to offer your bodies as a living sacrifice, holy and pleasing to God – this is your true and proper worship.

Okay, so this is huge.

"In view of God's mercy," writes Paul – in view of

---

1. "להאמין" in Hebrew, just in case you didn't believe me. Shame on you.

how lavish is His grace and how full His forgiveness and how endless His generosity – we should in turn "offer our bodies as *living* sacrifices." While that phrase could sound potentially scary, there's no need to panic. Paul emphasizes that God's looking for *living* sacrifices, which He finds both holy and pleasing to Himself. Importantly, Paul also identifies this process of offering our bodies as "living sacrifices" as *our true and proper worship.* This is big, because if you put these two verses together, Paul is ultimately saying that worship is comprised of two different things: ***glory and sacrifice.***

Glory and Sacrifice

First, what exactly are we referring to by the word "glory"? It's pretty straightforward; the word glory refers to giving great honor to someone or something, great praise and well-earned admiration and renown. It means to give credit where credit's due, and in God's case, it means that ultimate praise, full admiration and the highest of honors are richly deserved by the all-powerful, wise, majestic Creator from whom all things were conceived, through whom all things came and for whom they were created!

If God is not due great glory for what He's done and simply for who He is, I can't imagine who might be more deserving, amen? (Boom, there's that word!)

Now, as soon as you or I give glory to something, we're going to want to sacrifice to it. Some of you may be thinking, "That seems a little weird…" But stick with me. Paul clearly lays out the concept that the God of Heaven, who is due some serious glory, expects an appropriate level of sacrifice because of who He is. Back in the day (Christian slang for Old Testament times), living animals were sacrificed to atone for sins and to help people understand how glory and sacrifice were related. Now in New Testament times, Paul tells us God wants a *living* sacrifice. But either way, there's a definite connection in God's mind between giving something or someone glory and our willingness to make some kind of sacrifice to it.

Does that imply people tend to be worshippers? Actually, I'm not implying it. I'm straight up telling you:

people are worshippers. Using the Biblical concept of worship, you can see how this is true. Everyone seems to have someone or something that they have decided to 1) give glory and 2) sacrifice for. On that basis, it's not a matter of whether or not you worship. Whether you're a Christian, non-Christian, stubbornly agnostic, a believer in voodoo, enjoying dancing around Stonehenge or whatever, **everyone** is hardwired to worship, and literally, everyone ultimately does.[2]

> *People are worshippers... everyone is hardwired to worship, and literally everyone ultimately does.*

As an example, for some guys, their object of worship is their local sports team. I live near Baltimore, Maryland, and I can assure you that there are (reasonably) sane people who will, given the least provocation, worship the Ravens.

---

2. Are there people who decide no one is worthy of glory except themselves? Actually, they make the worship cut too; what they're into is self-glorification (and you can usually hear it when you chat with them) and they'll easily sacrifice on their own behalf and needs. Ah, but how about the guy who's "above it all" and simply will not give glory to anyone or sacrifice *anything*? I'm going to guess he's giving glory to his own willpower and individuality, and he's willing to sacrifice being misunderstood and proud for the way he simply won't "get with the crowd" and "be like the rest." And you can hear *that* in his voice, too. I know this is a long footnote, but you can handle it.

This just means that they give the Ravens great glory and don't mind making sacrifices for the team. And it's not just the Ravens; there are, likewise, tons of people who worship the Baltimore Orioles. (Oddly enough, there are also a few people who worship the Washington Redskins, although this is admittedly a stretch. But I digress...) Actually, in all seriousness, you may want to accuse me of exaggerating when I use the term "worship." Fair enough, but let's hold it up to the Biblical concept of the term:

Do these folks hold these teams in a place of ultimate glory? Yup.

Are they willing to cheerfully be "living sacrifices" for their team? Yup again.

How do they sacrifice, and in particular, do they actually make their bodies a "living sacrifice?" This question deserves a practical answer, because as people, we routinely and willingly "sacrifice" ourselves in many ways on behalf of that which we hold in high esteem and ultimately glorify. Notice I'm *not* saying it's all bad by any stretch. I'm just saying we need to acknowledge that we do this.

For example, we'll gladly sacrifice our time to that which we glorify. Using our sports analogy, we'll gladly sacrifice an opportunity to make some money in order to *spend* money to go and watch the objects of our worship shoot hoops or play football.[3] We'll sacrifice the time we might spend with our family in order to watch our team go at it. We'll sacrifice energy we didn't even know we *had* for the glory of our team, and at the end of the day, we will talk (and talk, and talk) incessantly about why the object of our worship is so worthy of glory – sometimes passionately, occasionally obnoxiously, every now and then even violently. We want people to know why the object of our worship is worth every bit of sacrifice we offer it. To be honest, I even know people who will routinely sacrifice their *dignity*, up to and including painting themselves into human flags at a ballgame.

And obviously, it's not just glory and sacrifice for sports teams. People glorify and sacrifice for Hollywood stars, political parties, automobiles, their newest tattoo,

---

3. Talking American football here people, not soccer. Just sayin'.

indie bands, cute chicks, hot guys, big bank accounts, ripped bodies, all kinds of drugs, cheap alcohol, expensive liquor, gourmet food and fast food junk – you name it, we worship it – all because it's hard-wired into the human psyche. You and I are going to worship *something,* so it's very much worth spending a little time to make sure we worship the **right thing.**

Okay, so hold up. Does this mean holding *anything* in high esteem or giving anything a place of honor is bad?

Absolutely not!

God loves to bless His

> *Anytime you take a good thing and make it a god-thing, it becomes a bad thing.*

people. The only way we can turn His blessing into a bad thing is when we forget Who gave us the blessing in the first place! We have the ability to transform a blessing into an idol (a false god) when we begin to put it first and sacrifice to it instead of God. Stated differently, anytime you take a good thing and make it a god-thing, it becomes a bad thing. There is a place in our hearts that is to be reserved for the true God and Him alone, not the little gods that we tend to make.

This is precisely why worship is not some dry, stoic religious ceremony. Worship is not a prayer recited from memory. It's not limited to a church service, a spiritual song or an exuberant act of praise. Worship in its purest form is the natural, grateful and humble outflow of honor and sacrifice from the heart of man after meeting the Truth of the Person of Jesus Christ.

That's why worship can be time spent with your kids, as long as we're thankful to God for the gift that is. Worship can also be done while enjoying an excellent steak at your favorite restaurant, provided we're grateful for the food and the experience.[4] Worship can be time alone by the sea shore, as we lift up our hearts to the very Creator of the sea. Worship can be doing work around the house as we're expressing appreciation for our homes to Him. And worship can be just you and God at rush hour, provided you don't lose your cool and yank somebody out of their car.

---

4. Or for you Vegans, some freshly roasted asparagus and some crisp, crunchy beets. Dang, doesn't that sound delicious? For me... I'm going with the steak.

What's the Purpose?

So then, if God really did hardwire us with a proclivity towards worship, a logical question at this point would be – what's the purpose of worship? *Why* did God make us this way?

And here's an unspoken question that sometimes pops into our minds, "could it be, (we sort of suspect but won't actually say) that God is a bit of an egotist?" "Could it be that He is somewhat 'needy', and that's why He requires all this attention or '*worship*'?" "Why does He need glory, anyway?" "Is there some kind of divine egotism at play?" We're told point blank in the Scripture that we're to "love the LORD your God with all your heart, all your soul and all your strength."[5] Wow, that's a mighty tall

> *Worship in its purest form is the natural, grateful and humble outflow of honor and sacrifice from the heart of man after meeting the Truth of the Person of Jesus Christ.*

_____

5. Deuteronomy 6:5

order! Is that even fair for Him to ask for it? Why on earth would God require such a thing?

Well, going back to our chapter on truth, God tells us very kindly that He doesn't technically need *anything* from us. As in, absolutely <u>nothing</u>. He's completely, eternally and infinitely complete within Himself, and always will be. There's no secret need in Him, God is certainly not lonely, and He never gets bored or insecure. So it can't be need, egotism or arrogance.

Why then the command for us to worship Him? The answer to the question is found by studying the rationale for worship. As we've learned, whatever we worship, we're going to give glory to, and whatever we're willing to give glory to, we're going to make sacrifices for it. Doesn't matter if it's a possession, money, sex, or whatever – we're going to give it glory, and we're going to sacrifice our time, energy, and money on its behalf. On top of that, we're going to talk about it. Actually, we're probably going to talk about it a lot. We love to talk about our object of worship.

And the reason we talk about it and discuss our passion is because we actually are designed to ***find joy in***

our worship. Worship has the potential to magnify and expand the joy we find in the object of worship! C.S. Lewis once wrote, "I think we delight to praise what we enjoy because the praise not merely expresses but completes the enjoyment."[6]

So the first obvious reason that God desires our worship is because He's worthy and He deserves it. **It's for Him**. But the second reason God desires our worship is because *worship fills us with joy*. **It's for us**. When we talk about God's goodness – reminding ourselves of all He's done – and become living sacrifices, we actually receive joy from it! It completes the experience of delighting in Him. So, when God calls us to worship, it's far from arrogance or some kind of divine neediness, it's actually divine *compassion* on our behalf and yet another expression of God's great love for us! God is not lonely, He's simply being mindful of how He created us and wants us to relate to Him as our Creator. That's a huge part of worship and a huge privilege, to build a relationship with the One who created us.

---

6. C.S. Lewis, *Reflections on the Psalms.*

What's the Result?

Finally, if that's the reason God requires our worship, can we expect any lasting results from worshiping? The answer can be kind of scary, because when you decide to offer something or someone your worship, you actually give it the power to change you. This can, of course, be either good or bad.

For example, if you worship money, you're going to naturally become more focused on it and greedy for more of it. Little by little, this will change you and me, and not for the better, because the worship of money is a false, dead end destination. It's idol worship, Jesus strongly condemned it, and if you prioritize money, glorify and offer your sacrifices to it, rest assured it will certainly change you.

Another example: if you give glory and sacrifice to a drug habit, it will change you. You'll gradually become more shallow and more intensely driven in horrific ways to sacrifice for it (I know this all too well from personal experience). Again, it's an idol and after requiring you to sacrifice your time and money, your relationships and family, the idol may require you to sacrifice your life. King David knew that worshiping various idols had the power to change us and wrote of them in the Psalms: "those who make [idols] become like them; so do all who trust in them."[7]

There are many negative examples of this process, but fortunately, and somewhat incredibly, the worship process is really **designed for our benefit and actually helps us** become more like Jesus. In fact, if you want to become more like Jesus, you *must become a worshipper of Jesus.* This means you must know Him, you must follow him, you must give Him glory in your heart, and you must be prepared to make sacrifices on His behalf – living sacrifices of time and money and energy and effort.

> *The worship process is really designed for our benefit and actually helps us become more like Jesus.*

And when you do?

You'll naturally become more kindhearted. Less proud. More generous. Quick to forgive, slow to anger, far less angry and increasingly more compassionate and loving toward others. It's really nothing short of a miracle, and yet we

---

7. Psalm 115:8

see it all the time in the true followers of Jesus. That's why it's so critical that the object of your worship must first have these qualities – love, humility, goodness, patience, forgiveness, wisdom, compassion, strength, loyalty and so forth – which unquestionably Jesus does, and so *much* much more. After all, if He wasn't loving, kindhearted, humble, quick to forgive, slow to anger, and full of compassion, He would have never forgiven people like you and me of our enormous sin debt.

When we know the truth, it sets us free. When we understand that Jesus is the Way, the Truth and the Life, it sets us free to trust Him and follow Him. And when we see that "God was pleased to have the fullness of His glory dwell in Jesus,"[8] this in turn sets us free and encourages us to give Him the glory He deserves, to present ourselves as living sacrifices to Him, and to express our love to Him through our worship. In the worship of Jesus, we experience a joy that we were not only created to experience, but can ultimately – and fortunately – find nowhere else.

It's easy. It's straightforward. And it's so simple.

---

8. Colossians 1:19

Think About It.

1. Has this chapter changed your perspective on worship? What other definitions of worship have you heard or held?

2. Given that everyone worships, what are some things or people that our culture worships? How does this correspond with Exodus 20:3?

3. What are the implications of Paul describing our lives as "living" sacrifices?

4. How is God's love for us expressed in His desire for our worship? In light of this, why is God "jealous" for our praise (Exod. 34:14)?

5. Since worship can take place anywhere we express awe and thankfulness towards God, what are some places or activities that stir you to worship?

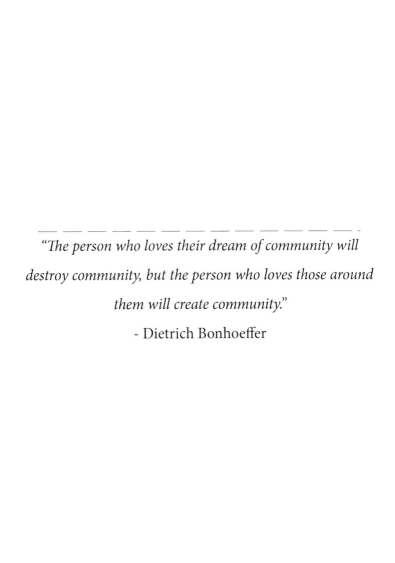

"*The person who loves their dream of community will destroy community, but the person who loves those around them will create community.*"

- Dietrich Bonhoeffer

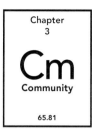

One of the most defining characteristics of modern western man is his insistence on individualism. We in the West tend to see ourselves as autonomous people who go through life as free-thinking, sovereign entities, with the emphasis on "sovereign." This is because of the underlying assumption that an individual's interests must come first. We want our own space, our own stuff and want to be our "own man." We want this to the extent that our individualism has even flavored Christianity in the West. In fact, the root of individualism is part of the phenomenon known as the "lone wolf" Christian, who professes to be a follower of Jesus but feels zero compulsion to be part of a church community. Lone wolves will often, sometimes loudly, trace their disinterest in all things church-related back to some negative experience or some perceived injustice by either a church body, church staffer or fellow attendee. Not all of it is imagination, but at the bottom of the root of individualism is the mistaken assumption that God's work of redemption is performed almost exclusively on an individual level.

Now, check this out. As far as I'm concerned, one of the most majestic and fascinating creations on this planet is the California redwood. These gigantic trees line portions of the northwest coast of the United States. Some of them sprouted as far back as twenty-five *hundred* years ago. This means some of these things – still alive today – were seedlings when the Greek Empire was in full swing – that's 500 years before Jesus!

That's impressive! Now, add to that not only are the redwoods some of the oldest things on earth, they are the unqualified tallest tree species in the world. Some of them can reach a high of three hundred feet in the sky.[1] For a little

---

1. I say "sky" because in my mind, at three hundred feet, you're no longer just in the air, you're in the sky. It may not be scientific but I'm going with it.

perspective, this is the same height as the Statue of Liberty. These are obviously some big trees.

At this point, you're wondering, "Paul… why are you talking about trees?"

I feel ya. Here's why.

You would probably assume, just like I did, that a California redwood at three hundred feet tall and with a life span measured in centuries must be anchored – in very, very deeply. After all, the thing weighs over 2 *million pounds.*

It better have some extremely deep roots.

But in fact, it doesn't.

Redwoods have a relatively shallow root system. What actually keeps the tree upright is that its root system is designed by God to intertwine with all the other redwoods nearby. Redwood roots spread wider and wider, not deeper and deeper. This creates an incredibly strong support system that allows these massive trees to sustain the powerful storms that cross the coast, complete with high winds and heavy rain. It's surprising, but a set of deep, individual roots are not what keep the redwoods upright. The real key to their survival is that the roots spread out underground, and the entire forest floor is interwoven like a grid.

The Promise of Jesus

I think the redwoods give us an exceedingly clear picture of a Jesus-centered community. And just so we understand, the community Jesus had in mind was an interwoven community of believers that undergird and support one another much like the redwoods. He made it clear that it was part of His mission to build exactly that kind of community.

This is why you read in Matthew's gospel how Jesus gathered His disciples together and asked them point-blank who they thought He was. Finally, at the climax of the conversation, Jesus posed the question to Simon Peter, to which Peter replied, "You are the Christ, the Son of the Living God."[2] Jesus immediately responded, "Simon, son of

2. Matthew 16:16

Bar-Jonah, flesh and blood has not revealed this to you, but my Father in heaven. And upon this rock..." – in other words, on that confession of Peter, on the statement that Jesus is the Christ, the Messiah, the Savior, the Son of God – "I am going to build my church, and the gates of Hell will not prevail against it."[3] There's a real excitement in this immediate and powerful answer from Jesus!

Ultimately, Jesus promised that it was His intention to build a different kind of community. Not a bunch of lone wolves who check in with each other at Christmas and Easter, but a real, thriving, community. And not just any community – He was talking about a community of actual believers, those who follow Him; a community destined to both storm the gates of Hell and to make a major, major impact in this world for His Kingdom. Jesus said clearly that this is what

> *Jesus promised that it was His intention to build a community. Not a bunch of lone wolves who check in with each other at Christmas and Easter, but a real, thriving, community.*

---

3. Matthew 16:17-18

He set out to build. It's worth noting that the same way Jesus established Truth was the same way He established worship. Now, we see Him about to establish a radically different form of community which the world had never seen – the Church. This was His intention and His idea all along. It's not something we came up with.

Fast forward to the very early parts of the Acts of the Apostles, and we'll see that Jesus had ascended back into Heaven and commissioned those same disciples to carry on His mission. It's really no wonder that we immediately get a very clear picture of this interlocking system of roots already beginning to grow. The Book of Acts begins by showing how this type of community began to take shape. It says that they (and this is the church now) "devoted themselves to the Apostles teaching, and to fellowship, to the breaking of bread, and to pray. Everyone was filled with awe of the many wonders and signs performed by the Apostles."[4]

Now, watch this.

"All of the believers were together, and they had everything

---

4. Acts 2:42-43

in common. They sold property and possessions to give to anyone who had need, and every day they continued to meet together in the temple courts. They broke bread and they ate together with glad and sincere hearts, praising God and enjoying the favor of all the people."[5]

Sounds beautiful to me, but how do we know it was beautiful to God?

"And as a result," the Bible says, " the Lord added to their number daily those who were being saved."[6]

This is exactly what true, Jesus-centered community looks like. And if you're looking for a good working definition for community, try this: Christian Community is a group of people who are following Jesus together, doing life together and strengthening each other, so that they can fulfill His mission together.

Simple.

> *Christian Community is a group of people who are following Jesus together, doing life together and strengthening each other, so that they can fulfill His mission together.*

_____

5. Acts 2:44-45

6. Acts 2:47

The Purpose of Community

In this passage, there's a few details that deserve a little closer look.

First, they devoted themselves to the Apostles teaching, which is another way of saying that the community learned about Jesus. Because the community recognizes Jesus as the Truth, it has to be centralized around His written Word. This is why in healthy, vibrant churches, community is based on studying Jesus, learning about Jesus, and reading about Jesus. This very naturally inspires us to pray to Jesus in an effort to understand what He wants for us. The focus here is to know not just more *about* Jesus, but to actually *know* Jesus. We can do this by spending time in His word. This is exactly why at Lighthouse, the pursuit of Truth is one of our core elements. Jesus said pretty directly that He is the beginning and the end[7]; therefore, we make Him *our* beginning, the same way that the first church in history did.

Next, the early church did life together. If you're

_____

7. Revelation 22:13

not down with Christian lingo, this simply means that early Christians hung out together. Biblical, Jesus-centered community means that we're going to do life together. This can admittedly get messy, because you and I naturally bring the mess. You don't even have to think about it. People are messy! We're physically messy, emotionally messy, even spiritually messy sometimes. But if you've got small kids or have been around them for more than ten minutes, you already know life is messy. And we're no different. If we're really a community, messy or not, we're going to hang out, we're going to go to the ball game, we're gonna do dinner, I'm going to watch your kids when I don't really feel like it, I'm going to listen to your problems and you're going to help me solve mine. It might be that our kids are involved in the same sports or that we're entering rehab together. One way or another, we're going to do life together. These first century Christians actually *liked* each other and they hung out together. This is precisely why we do small groups here at Lighthouse Church, because we are faithful to Jesus' original plan for the church which was (and is) to make it a Jesus-centered community.

Furthermore, when they did this – they encouraged each other to see Jesus at work everywhere. After studying the word and hanging out till all hours, everyone was being encouraged and filled with awe at the many wonders and signs that were being performed by Jesus through the Apostles. Now in that day some *crazy* miracles were happening every time you turned around. They were witnessing healings and events that simply couldn't be explained outside of the supernatural intervention of God. And the people were blown away by it.

I'm happy to say at Lighthouse Church, by God's good grace, we have the privilege of witnessing miracles of conversions and signs of growth in new believers and wonders in the lives of those who are following Him. Miracles don't flow exclusively through pastors, elders, leaders or Apostles. Miracles can flow through you! Growth, conversion, truth and life are taking place within His community. It's a miracle when people are meeting Jesus and being saved. It's a miracle marriages are being reconciled. It's a miracle when addictions are being broken and when renewal is daily taking place. Babies are being born (*lots* of babies, actually) finances are being provided, emotional wounds are being healed and the list goes on. And in a fallen world where bad news is usually the norm, people see this happening in community and are naturally in awe over it, because it's a miracle!

It gets even better! Acts continues that all the believers were together and they had everything in common. Because they were eager to share the love of Jesus, they were eager to share their stuff! They shared their homes, their money, their food, their time and their energy – they willingly and purposely gave of themselves and shared their lives so that they could strengthen the other "redwoods." They sustained those who didn't have enough – enough time, enough money, enough food, enough faith. They were willing to contribute to the family of God, naturally and organically, the same way that reasonably healthy and functional families do all the time. The Scripture says that they even sold property and possessions to give to those who were in need. It's clear. They put their money where their mouth was. Obviously, this is not something "lone wolves" can or will do, and as a result, they sadly miss out on the joy that community provides.

You know what this means? This means that your

problem should become a little bit of my problem. It means I should be willing to make your burden become a little bit of my burden. It also means I should be willing to make my blessing become a blessing for you, and my excess should become your provision. This is exactly how the early Christians looked at Jesus-centered community. They went as far as actually selling their stuff to take care of one another. When Acts tells us that every day they met in the temple courts, it basically means they went to church together.

> *Hearts that are devoted to Jesus will be devoted to a Jesus-centered community.*

They would meet at church, but then they would head back to their homes and eat together " with glad and sincere hearts."[8] I mean, these people were legitimately happy! They were happy in community, and they loved one another. They went and worshipped Jesus out of sheer joy, followed by a good meal, a little corn hole and then the Ravens game[9] to

---

8. Act 2:46

9. You know what I'm saying.

close the evening out. They enjoyed life simply because Jesus was at the center of it.

They were joyful. Why shouldn't they be? They were exuberant for every good reason. This is a faithful group of people who made a point to learn about Jesus, do life together, help each other see His work everywhere, share His love by sharing their resources and attend church together like a family. And Acts 2:47 notes that "the LORD then added to their number daily those who were being saved."

To the lone wolves out there, let me just say this. Either you have said, or have heard it said, "I love Jesus. I just don't like the church."

Well, that's whack.

Here's why: If you say that you like me but don't like my wife, then you and I have a problem. Ruth and I are a package deal; Scriptures says we're actually one flesh. In the same way, if you say that you love Jesus but not His church, you are saying you love Jesus

> *When a community can love each other because they love Him first... Jesus will add to a community like that.*

but not His bride. Jesus laid His life down for His church; we better treat it with the same respect and care that He does, or we risk showing disrespect to His precious bride that He's coming back for one day soon.

See, I'm convinced that as 2nd Chronicles 16:9 says, "the eyes of the Lord go to and fro throughout the whole earth, seeking hearts that are devoted to Him." I wholeheartedly believe that those whose hearts are devoted to Jesus will be devoted to a Jesus-centered community. And when we champion community in the way Scripture calls us to, I believe Jesus will continue to add to that community.

It's the heart of our Savior to adopt sons and daughters, to forgive their sins and to place them in communities and families that are healthy, happy and focused on Him. This is what happens when the church is functioning like the church is supposed to; when a community can love each other because they love Him first. Jesus will add to a community like that, one that's following Him together, doing life together and strengthening each other, so that they can fulfill His mission together. He's already done it in the Book of Acts.

He's still doing it today.

<u>Think About It.</u>

1. Do you think the advent of social media has strengthened or hurt community in our culture?

2. Is it possible for non-believers to experience true community?

3. Think of a time you experienced community with other believers. What were the components of that experience? What did that experience have that churches struggling to achieve community may lack?

4. How does the doctrine of the Trinity broaden our understanding of God's view on community?

5. How can churches which are full of broken, hurting and imperfect people have community? How do love and forgiveness factor in church community?

"The life of Christ was a life of humble simplicity, yet how infinitely exalted was his mission. Christ is our example in all things."

- Ellen G. White

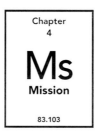

Chapter
4

Ms

Mission

83.103

James Hudson Taylor wasn't really a remarkable man.

At least, not at first. James was just a normal guy who in his late teens knew Jesus, loved Jesus and walked with Jesus. There came a day in his walk with the Lord that Taylor's heart for evangelism to the people of China began to stir. Taylor responded in obedience[1] and was eventually moved by God to make evangelism to the people of China his life's mission. He really wanted nothing more – and nothing less – than to communicate the Gospel of Jesus Christ to them.

So, he moved to China. This was no small thing, moving to China; it took him a very dangerous six months

1. Also, he immediately started studying Mandarin Chinese, Hebrew, Greek and Latin. Dude was no slouch. http://en.wikipedia.org/wiki/Hudson_Taylor

just to get there. After he arrived, Taylor found that he could more easily reach the Chinese if he dressed more like them. It was a little weird, a white dude dressing like the Chinese dudes, but he felt called to do it. So, he did.

He also starting eating in the places where the locals would eat[2] and hung out where the locals hung out – very different approach from the cultural isolation of the more traditional missionary efforts of the late 1800s. The entire time he was doing this, he was the recipient of a steady stream of ridicule and pushback from his former peers who had now become some of his greatest critics for "going too far" to share the Gospel with the Chinese.

Was his strategy radical? Definitely.

But was it effective? You tell me.

After spending 51 years in China and founding the China Inland Mission, it's widely accepted that Taylor's efforts resulted in a minimum of 800 missionaries going to China who began 125 schools. This led to the direct conversion of over 18,000 people as well as the establishment of more

---

2. Never really a bad idea, for the record.

than 300 stations of work with over 500 helpers covering all eighteen provinces of China.[3] All of this plus the **hundreds of thousands of subsequent conversions** both in China and throughout the world paints a pretty clear picture of the success of James Hudson Taylor's willingness to sell out to the Mission of Jesus.

See, James was clear that he had met the Truth and His name was Jesus. He then clearly understood that his life should be given to the worship of Jesus. He also surrounded himself with healthy Community that spurred him on in his faith. And James knew there was nothing left to do but to try to win as many people as possible to the same freedom that he had found in Jesus. He was now clear on what his overriding priority in life had to be: **to fulfill the Mission of Jesus Christ.**

There are many similarities between James Hudson Taylor and the Apostle Paul, particularly their focus on mission. Paul said to the early church in Acts chapter 20, "But nothing, not even my life, is more important than

---

3. http://en.wikipedia.org/wiki/Hudson_Taylor

my completing my mission. This is nothing other than the ministry I received from the Lord Jesus to testify about the good news of God's grace."[4]

This is so simple and the same pattern as James Hudson Taylor! First, Paul meets Jesus Who is the Truth on the road to Damascus. Next, he clearly understands that Jesus is God and is therefore worthy of glory and sacrifice – in other words, worship. Then, Paul surrounded himself with Christian community, and finally, he gives himself over to the Mission of Jesus. Paul knew in his heart that he needed to win as many as possible to the same gospel of freedom with which he had been blessed. Paul *had* to fulfill the Mission. He lived with the unshakable belief that *today* had to be spent anticipating a far greater Day – the great and awesome day of our King's final return.

The Great reformer, Martin Luther, operated under the same principle. Luther knew about the Mission of Jesus Christ, and he understood that life was supposed to be invested in the fulfillment of that Mission. At one point he

4. Acts 20:24

essentially said, "Really, there's only two days that matter. We live *this* day, for *That Day*." Martin got it, just like the Apostle Paul and just like James Hudson Taylor – life is to be spent on mission.

But what we often do is we make fulfilling the mission way more complicated then it should be. We convolute it like we do with almost everything else. We add to the simplicity of what Jesus told us to do. We take things away. We add things to it. And we manage to leave ourselves tired before we even get started, overwhelmed before we even take the first step. We end up taking something that should be refreshing and exciting and somehow transform it into something tedious and fatiguing.

What Jesus simply wanted done was for His followers to go and tell others about His good news. Not in some weird way or some super spiritual method that winds up freaking people out but in a way that's normal, life giving and compelling! Jesus is all of that, so why wouldn't His message be the same? And in so doing, people are going to be saved! From there we **teach them to worship, include them in a healthy community and get them on Mission**

with us. In other words, we're to **reach the lost, and make disciples**.[5] What Paul knew, James Hudson Taylor knew, Luther knew, and we need to know – the Mission is to reach the lost, and make disciples. This is the same Mission Jesus gave His disciples, and it's the same Mission He gives to us. It's not complicated! But, unfortunately that's what we make it.

Let me give you an embarrassing example.

I remember one time my wife needed me to go to the store. She needed paper plates, romaine lettuce and that was it. She asked me, "Will you go get these two things on your way home from work?" Husband extraordinaire that I am, I said "No prob, I got it." I jumped into my car and drove to Safeway. Upon entering, I immediately got sidetracked. Seriously… I'm not sure exactly how it happens, but it happens all the time! I remember it was a winter day, because I was surprised when I walked in and there they were in front of me: a wooden pallet full of cherries. Even though they were selling for around 4 million dollars a pound, I just couldn't

---

5. New International Foster Version (a.k.a. my paraphrase of Matthew 16:19-20.)

resist, and I wind up grabbing a bag of them. I did this in the full knowledge that I was probably going to have to steal money from my daughter to pay for them or delay payment on things less important than cherries, like electricity. Next, like every time I go to the grocery store, I wind up in the seafood aisle, staring at the lobster tails. Of course, seafood is never really far from the fresh meat, so next thing I did was spend a few minutes watching my man carve up some prime rib. This particular day I hit the jackpot: lobster tails are half off, so I got two for ten bucks. I collect my lobster, grab myself a steak, and I get Ruth one too after convincing myself that I was being a really good guy. I think I even got a small steak for the kids to split. My kids don't even like steak! I find the paper plates, pick up a starter log and head for the check out.

Now I'm out the door and on my way home, a) thinking what a terrific guy I actually was and b) feeling a little frustration about the amount of money I actually spent providing for my family. I walk into the kitchen, still feeling a little edgy. I dump everything on the counter and proceed to inform Ruth that she was *not* to send me to the grocery store any more, because "we're spending too much money." Meanwhile, Ruth is unloading the lobster tails, the steaks, the starter log and the paper plates. And with the cherries rolling around on the counter at about 3 bucks apiece, Ruth looks up at me and says, "Paul, but you *didn't even get the lettuce*!"

Talk about frustrating! We've got lobster tails we don't need, steak we don't want and cherries we can't afford. And the end result was – Ruth frustrated, me frustrated, kids frustrated. The lobsters were probably frustrated too. Who knows? All because I complicated a simple mission to just grab some paper plates and some lettuce.

Unfortunately, this is sometimes what we do with the Mission Jesus gives us. We add to, take away and grab some cherries along the way. Next thing you know we've decided to "improve" the Mission by doing a little less of this and a little more of that, eventually driving us and everybody around us insane and leaving ourselves exhausted and frustrated. God tells us to get some lettuce, and we bring him lobster. Why?

We're just not operating in simplicity.[6] With that in mind, let's look at a few things we need to understand about simple, Jesus-centered Mission.

Jesus Came for Us

First, the only reason that we're able to even perform the Mission is that Jesus first came on mission for us. Luke 19:10 tells us that "the Son of Man came to seek and to save the lost." This is the Gospel. To point out the glaringly obvious, you and I were the lost items that He came looking for. You, I and billions of others are people that *Jesus personally came to seek out and save*. He sought us out when we were still His enemies (many of us in open defiance), and He saved our wretched souls and made us sons and daughters. Jesus came on mission for us. We're told that He died for the sake of all so that those who are alive

> *Love motivated His rescue Mission and still motivates Him today.*

---

6. You *did* read the first chapter, right?

should not live for themselves but for the One who died for them.[7] Why? **Because He is absolutely in love with us.** *I mean He really loves us.* Love motivated His rescue Mission and still motivates Him today.

This is the sole reason that I can write down the words of this book and mean it. Because the Truth came after me first. There was a time in my life when I was totally lost. I was strung out on heroin, wanting nothing to do with God, whacked out, jacked up, mad at the church and mad at my parents for no reason other than my selfish, wicked heart. The whole time I was the beneficiary to a practically perfect up-bringing.

I had reached a point where I was 19 years old and scared for my life. I was close to 6 feet tall and weighed all of 135 pounds soaking wet. My heroin use was now using me. It was bad, *very bad*. After much arguing and resisting (with people who loved me) my obvious need for help, I finally caved in and agreed to go to a Christian-centered rehab called Teen Challenge. My intention was

---

7. 2 Corinthians 5:15

to go, commit to this year long program and then dip out after only 2 weeks. All I wanted to accomplish was a quick detox, some weight gain and to move past the immediate threat of death.

But Jesus showed up and wrecked all of that!

As I was on my bed one hot July night about 2 weeks in, I was planning my exit strategy for the following day. See, it was Friday night and on Saturday I was allowed one ten minute phone call. I was going use that call to have someone come pick me up. In my mind, I was done. I had detoxed, and I had packed on a whole 8 pounds (I had been doing push ups twice a day, so I thought I looked beast). I thought I had got what I came for.

But as I lay there thinking about where I was going to go the following day, something happened that would forever change my life. Jesus came to me. Not physically. I'm not some weirdo. But in all reality, He came to me![8] And He said to me as clear as day:

"Paul, you find out how awesome I am and you'll fear

---

8. This is no time to get weird, so stick with me.

me. And when you fear me you'll obey me. And when you obey me you'll fall in love with me."

That succession of statements ran over and over again in my mind. It was like I couldn't stop hearing it. So much so that I finally sat up and wrote it down. To be honest, I wasn't blown away with *what* Jesus spoke to me. (Frankly, I didn't even know what it meant. But I would soon understand.) It was more that He came to me!! There I was, full of arrogance and pride and fully convinced that I – this strung out addict – knew everything about everything. Then, the King of the Universe came after me in downtown Washington D.C. I couldn't even believe that He would give me the time of day, let alone chase me down. But He did, and I have never been the same. I ended up spending over a year in that program and never have looked back.

Jesus' rescue Mission for Paul Samuel Foster?

Undeniably successful.

And I'm just one out of countless people who were personally sought out and rescued by our great Hero and Savior Jesus.

Jesus Sends Us on Mission

Does it end with the rescue? Of course not. That's why once He has redeemed us, Jesus sends us on mission for others. This is why John 20:21 says, "Again Jesus said, peace be with you." What every Christian finds out is that the "peace" part of that statement actually *is* Jesus.[9] He continues saying, "As the Father sent me, I am sending you."

Pretty straightforward, isn't it? This is what we get saved into – a mission of going after others and creating in them a hunger and a thirst to be part of the family of God. We go out on mission the same way He went out on mission. This is also why Acts 17:24 indicates that Jesus, in His great wisdom and knowledge, has positioned us in the very times and circumstances in which we should live, such as the communities we live in and the jobs we perform,

> *Jesus is building His church and strategically sets His sons and daughters in place for mass impact.*

_____

9. In the same manner that He is the Way, the Truth, and the Life. John 11:2 also tells us He is the Resurrection!

so that we can be His tool to reach lost people. So, friends… if you've ever wondered why the heck you're living in beautiful Glen Burnie and why you work at Wal-Mart, the answer is – because you probably made some serious mistakes along the way! Nah, just kidding… **The real answer is because Jesus is building His church and strategically sets His sons and daughters in place for mass impact**. All of this is ordained so that men and women that are far from Him but who He is drawing to Himself *can find Him through us being on mission*.[10]

This is huge! Jesus finds us in our destructive, self-centered train wrecks of lives, introduces Himself and then graciously provides us with Truth. Not some weird subjective truth and not some politically correct relativistic truth but the real, God's-eye TRUTH. Then, He overhauls our understanding of worship, kicks out all the false gods we've been glorifying and sacrificing to and gives us a real joy in the process. Are we then left to our devices? Heck no!

---

10. Jesus includes us in His Mission out of generosity and grace. Obviously he doesn't *need* our help, but He loves our help, the same way I don't necessarily *need* my son Asher's help repairing the lawnmower, but I sure love working with him.

Jesus sees to it that we're led into a good, solid, Jesus-centered community and then finally sends us out on mission to ask other to join us. This is nothing short of our life's purpose.

Jesus Equips Us for the Mission

Third, Jesus equips us to fulfill the Mission. This could probably be an entirely different book, so I'll keep this brief.[11] It's shown throughout the Gospels that Jesus would routinely send out His disciples who were basically a bunch of ragtag, roughneck fishermen, tax collectors and people you would generally want to keep an eye on while your valuables were around. These were some previously shady cats, and most of these guys were on the ragged edges of society. Somehow, this ends up being the crew that God, in His sovereignty, decides to send out on Mission to rescue the world. I love it!

Then, to underscore His sufficiency, as they're on their way out the door to rescue the world, He tells them to

---

11. Yes, I'm capable.

not even bother taking anything with them. Like, nothing! He told them to skip the spare clothes, not to worry about the money and actually went so far as to tell them to not even worry about what they were *going to say*, because he was going to tell them what to say when they arrived. This is why Matthew 28:20 says, "And I will be with you until the very end of the earth." Jesus is so motivated that we fulfill the Mission that we're told He will personally and fully equip us to bring about impact regardless of our ability.

Jesus is Coming Back

Lastly, just at the point that we need some energy boosting motivation, we're reminded that Jesus is going to come back for us on a pickup Mission. This is one of the coolest things in the whole Bible to me. Now, I know we live in turbulent, crazy, whacked out times. And I know that at any given moment, practically anything can happen. I also know that many people live in fear and anxiety. And we could talk about how bad things are till the cows come home, but we – the adopted, rescued children of the Living God –

are personal friends[12] with the Hope of the world. And one day Jesus is going to come back to this battle-scarred planet and deliver us into a world where **all things have been made new** – brand spankin new! In this new world, no one's going to be in debt, nobody's going to be in a bad mood, nobody's kids will be out of control or living at home in their late thirties. There won't be any car crashes or bounced checks. Specifically, Scripture says there won't be any more crying, no tears, no death or sickness. And I'm pleased to announce, there will be no more fear or anxiety, no more broken homes and no more broken hearts. Why? **Because Jesus is going to come back and fix everything.** Sound amazing? You better believe it is:

> *Then I saw heaven opened, and behold, a white horse! The one sitting on it is called Faithful and True, and in righteousness he judges and makes war. His eyes are like a flame of fire, and on his head are many diadems, and he has a name written that no one knows but himself. He is*

---

12. In John 15:15 Jesus indicates that He considers us His friends. Don't believe me? Look it up.

clothed in a robe dipped in blood, and the name by which he is called is The Word of God. And the armies of heaven, arrayed in fine linen, white and pure, were following him on white horses. From his mouth comes a sharp sword with which to strike down the nations, and he will rule them with a rod of iron. He will tread the winepress of the fury of the wrath of God the Almighty. On his robe and on his thigh he has a name written, King of kings and Lord of lords. (Rev. 19:11-16)

This is our great King Jesus. He's going to come back on His final rescue Mission. He's gonna come back, open a can and set the record straight once and for all **that He's The King of Kings and The Lord of Lords.** And *That Day* will be worth living for Jesus *this day.*

So Church, His Mission is what it's all about! It's the sole reason why Lighthouse Church exists. We are here to reach the lost and make disciples. And we don't carry a heavy burden like we've got to do it all, because we have it in writing that our King Jesus is blazing a trail ahead of us. He's drawing men and women to Himself, and He's stirring the hearts of men and women who are hopelessly lost. Our job is **simply to be faithful to Him and His Mission,** live "this day for That Day" and tell others about who He is and about His incredible work in our lives so that Jesus can use our testimony to lead others into brand new life with Him.

He's coming back on a rescue Mission for us! He's coming back to make all things new! And that's the day we're living for, because **Truth** is a person. **Worship** is our proper response. His **Community** is our family. And His **Mission** is our purpose.

It's simple. It's workable. It's proven. It's supernatural and it's God's plan for you to not only succeed in your walk with Him but to flourish and excel as a modern day disciple.

Let's wrap this up in the Epilogue.

<u>Think About It.</u>

1. What fear(s) cause you the most reservation to living a life on mission?

2. What personal strengths and giftings has God given you that you could use to live a life on mission?

3. Have you ever had an encounter where you shared Jesus with someone? What did you learn from that experience and what will you do different next time?

4. Read Acts 17:24-27. Where are you called to be on mission and who is God calling you to focus on?

5. Read Acts 20:24. What is your testimony of redemption and how can that be used as you live a life on mission?

Epilogue

Alright, we've worked through these elements together.

Now, here's my hope:

I hope that you would not walk way from this short book without a resolved direction or a resolved heart. Let's get real, many of us have some serious simplification that needs to be done in our lives. And with God's help, I know we're gonna do it!

But I'm talking about something else right now.

Primary Risk

See, there's one item area that must make it to the top of the priority list, and that's your relationship with Jesus.

What's at stake is huge. It's eternal. And there are two main risks that go with it.

One, if you don't have a relationship with Jesus, you're risking an eternity apart from God. This is the "wrath" part we talked about in the "Truth" chapter, and there are only two, very simple outcomes.

Your first option is to be in a right relationship with Jesus, with your sins paid for and your conscience clear. This is a really good place to be in this life and after it.

Second option is to remain a stranger to Jesus, with sins piling up left and right and God not one bit happy with the way you're ignoring Him and suppressing His Truth. This is a really bad place to be in life and a really, really bad place when life is finished.

The handling of this priority actually determines the eternal state of your soul! And I'm not being dramatic. Now, hear me. Personally, I'm not saying that I'd even set it up like this. It's a very stark choice with no grey area. But for whatever reason, God didn't consult me (oddly enough) when He created reality. This ain't my ice cream shop, and I'm not the boss. I just work here so listen up. God says you and I need to get this priority right. He says we must actually know Jesus and not just about Him. So, that's the first risk, and if you don't have this down, the risk to yourself is way way too high; your eternal state hangs in the balance.

Secondary Risk

The second risk is connected to the first. If you don't know Jesus, then you're not yet in touch with the Truth. Without the Truth, you're going to be tempted to worship all kinds of ridiculous and dangerous stuff, as we outlined in the Worship chapter. And even if you hook up with a Christian community somehow, without a good understanding of Truth or Worship, it'll really just be God's grace if you hang around for any length of time at all.

See how risky? Here's what's even riskier.

What happens when people go on mission without knowing Jesus?

Chaos happens.

Even with the best of intentions, these people can't teach the truth effectively because they don't know Him.

They can't encourage worship correctly, because they don't actually understand it. And they cannot be comfortable in community, because they think it should be somehow religious, instead of relational, Jesus-centered, healthy, refreshing and life-giving. People do this all the time.

And it can get even crazier, because if we don't know Jesus first, then we're naturally running the risk of misrepresenting Him to others! We also run the risk of not having a clue what our purpose is in life. This goes on and on. It's these kinds of risks that make it imperative that we first and foremost get in step with the simplicity of Jesus' priorities.

We get one shot at this life. And we've got to get this one right.

So, here's a few summary questions for you to ask yourself. Actually, I made it dummy proof and even gave you the answers.[1] These questions and answers can go a long way towards leading us to simplicity.

---

1. Why? Cause I love ya! Plus these are the kinds of tests I always liked taking.

Question: First, what is truth?

Answer: Truth is more than a concept or a proposition. Truth is a person. His name is JESUS.

Question: Second, what should be my object of worship to which I primarily sacrifice my time, energy, money, efforts and resources?

Answer: The object of our worship is the Creator of you, me and the rest of universe – He who loves us with an everlasting love. His name is JESUS.

Question: Third, what type of community is the healthiest and most pleasing to God for us to commit ourselves to?

Answer: We were designed to grow with a community of believers who are following Jesus together, doing life together and strengthening each other so that they can fulfill His mission together. At the center of the community is JESUS.

Question: Lastly, what's the Mission? What's the purpose of knowing the Truth, understanding Worship and serving through Community?

Answer: These things prepare us for being on mission for Jesus and to live unreservedly for the One who first came on a rescue mission for us. Then, we're to turn around and go on mission for others, ultimately telling them about Him, how He gave His life for us and rose again to give us the ability to experience true life. The One we're to tell others about is JESUS.

If you have a different answer to any of these 4 questions, here's what you need to do – get things straight with God before doing anything else. Again, you can't really understand the Truth, properly worship Him or feel like you're part of a community that's centered on Him until you have a relationship with Him.

To experience the fullness of Jesus, understand that God is fully ready, willing and able to forgive your sin and eager to restore your relationship with Him.[2] We have to humble ourselves, repent for our sin and then turn our lives

---

2. Isaiah 1:18 – "Come let us reason together says the LORD; though your sins are like scarlet, I will wash them white as snow."

over to Him.[3] We also need to acknowledge that the only way we could ever approach the Father Who now welcomes us as sons and daughters is through Jesus Who paid for our sins.[4] Ask Jesus to strengthen you and thank Him for His full forgiveness which He purchased FOR YOU on the cross!

Then, live it like you mean it! I mean really mean it! You were made for this! So, go ahead, read the truth of the Bible (His letter to you) and get to know Him better. Get rid of the pointless and dangerous little gods you've created in your life and follow and worship Him wholeheartedly. Next, find a community of equally sold out people and don't be too surprised when Jesus shows you where to serve and where you need to be served.

And then finally: GET ON MISSION!

Why? What do you mean, why? Weren't you paying

---

3. Act 3:19 – "Repent, then, and turn to God, so that your sins may be wiped out, that times of refreshing may come from the Lord"

4. 2 Corinthians 6:18 – "I will be a Father to you, and you will be my sons and daughters, says the Lord Almighty."

attention? Because time's short! The need is huge! The challenge is out there! You've been saved for a reason! And plus, we could sure use the help.

I'm looking forward to working with you. Thanks for reading this.

See you at church on Sunday!

Acknowledgements

This small piece of written work could have never been accomplished by my own effort. This came together as a result of an incredible team of people that I am truly blessed to work with. I want to say a huge thank you to the following people. If it were not for you guys, I'd still be staring at a blank screen.

Gordon Smart: Thank you so much for editing, giving great ideas and taking a mess, at times, and helping me make something of it. There's no way I could have done it without you.

Jesse Freeman: You are always on the receiving end of me sharing my crazy ideas and seldom telling me I'm crazy! You jump right in and help with the creativity ideas that take a simple idea to a "whole nutha level."

Tim Feeney: Man, you labor to make sure things are rooted deep in scripture and that whatever the project, Jesus is the focus. Thank you for helping to provide a Biblical foundation for these "Elements."

Steve Healy: You have been a blessing from the start. You always keep me and the project on task and make sure things are done with order with the church's benefit in mind. Love you man.

Ruth Foster: You're my best friend and hands down biggest cheerleader. Thank you for your patience over the life of this project giving me all the margin I needed to get it done. I sure love you and couldn't imagine doing life without you.

Love you guys!

Lighthouse Church

Simple church. Simply Jesus.

www.lighthouse.church